by Douglas Wootton
edited by Alison Hedger

A factual and amusing musical all about water
and the hydrologic cycle.

Suitable for children 5 to 9 years

Approximate duration 35 minutes

Teacher's Book complete with play, lyrics, music and matching CD
of all the music in the show.
Backing tracks are included for performances and rehearsals, as well as a
vocal version for learning purposes and demonstration.

SONGS

1. H_2O *Atoms*
2. A Wave Went Up My Nose *Seaside Children*
3. The Sun Has Said Goodbye To Mister Moon *All*
4. Fire Heats The Water *Singing Groups*
5. Snowflakes *Winter Children*
6. Jacky Jacky Jack Frost *Jack Frost and Ice Fairies*
7. The Hydrologic Cycle Rag *All*

© Copyright 2002 Golden Apple Productions
A division of Chester Music Limited
8/9 Frith Street, London W1D 3JB.

Order No. GA11308

ISBN 0-7119-9153-7

CAST LIST

Atoms: Hydrogen
    (twice as many as oxygen)
    Oxygen
They join up into groups of three, to make water molecules.

Water Molecules
Allocate one of the three children to speak where appropriate. If using capable children the three parts of each molecule could speak in chorus.

Seaside Children
Dressed for the beach with buckets and spades. They act out a swim routine and sing.

Sun
Speaking.

Sunbeams
Speaking and optional dancing.

Clouds
These are formed from the joining up of molecules. They carry cardboard cloud cut outs.

Mister Moon
Non speaking

Stars
Non speaking   } *optional extra parts*

Night
Non speaking

Groups of Singers
For Song 4 - 'FIRE HEATS WATER'
White shirts and blouses. Girls wear a frilly apron.
Each child carries a tea pot, jar of coffee etc.

Four Winds: **North**
                South
                East
                West
Wearing flowing chiffon scarves of different colours.
These children deliver poetry.

Television Weather Presenter
Speaking.

Snowflakes
Dance.

Winter Children
Dressed for cold weather. Singing.

Jack Frost
Non speaking.

Ice Fairies
Singing and optional dancing.

Group of Musicians
Optional, but could make all kinds of appropriate sound effects throughout the play and give rhythmic accompaniment to the songs.

Only minimal stage directions are given, leaving each producer to direct as he/she chooses. Several parts are optional and the cast can be tailored to suit your particular needs, bearing in mind the ages of the children involved. You may care to have Mister Moon, Stars and Night on stage to open, with suitable low level lighting and improvised accompanying percussion.

COSTUMES AND PROPS

Please devise your own costumes, as resources and time allow. Perhaps the hydrogen atoms should be blue, and the oxygen atoms white? Being covered in a balaclava, down to slippers in the colours chosen, would be fun! Teachers are full of imagination, and the author is in no doubt that creative ideas will flow. Other character costumes will be less demanding on the imagination.

Most of the props are given in the cast list. In addition you may care to explore the possibility of having weather maps and satellite pictures for the weather presenter.

Stage lighting is not required, but if it is available it always adds to the atmosphere.

EDUCATIONAL KEY WORDS

The following words are found in the script:

Oxygen	
Hydrogen	
H_2O	
Atoms	see script page 5
Water	
Molecule	
Evaporating	see script page 9
Boiling	
Precipitate	see script page 12
Snow	
Ice	see script page 13
Thaw	
Liquid	see script page 14

H_2O is pronounced "*aitch–two–oh*" throughout.

Oxygen Atoms: Hello everybody,
Stepping forward We're oxygen you know.

Hydrogen Atoms: And we're a gas called hydrogen.
Stepping forward Welcome to our show.

All Atoms: We're going to join together
To make some H_2O,
And tell you all about
The many places we can go.

Two Oxygen Atoms join up hands with a single Hydrogen Atom to make the first water molecule. The parts of this molecule speak . . .

Hydrogen Atoms: As you can see
Pointing to themselves There are two of us.

Oxygen Atom: And one of me, makes three.

Hydrogen Atoms: So two of us are hydrogen . . . *Pointing*

Oxygen Atom: And oxygen, that's me! *Pointing*

All Atoms: And we are little atoms,
Doing what we oughter.
'Cause when we're all joined up together
We make WATER!

All atoms group into threes; two hydrogen and one oxygen.

So listen very carefully
To our scientific rule:
H_2O (*say very slowly*) makes
A water molecule!

SONG ONE H_2O

Atoms: Water, water,
Water, water.   *(Clap or echo the word "water" after each word)*
H_2O is what we are,   } *twice*
H_2O clap hands, hurrah!
Though we are so very small
We can make a waterfall.
Joined together we can be
Rivers flowing to the sea.
H_2O is what we are,   } *twice*
H_2O clap hands, hurrah!
Water, water,
Water, water.   *(Clap or echo the word "water" after each word)*

H is for hydrogen,
Oxygen's O,
And there is water
Wherever we go.
H is for hydrogen,
Oxygen's O,
And when we meet
Crystal water will flow.

H_2O is what we are,   } *twice*
H_2O clap hands, hurrah!
Though we are so very small
We can make a waterfall.
Joined together we can be
Rivers flowing to the sea.
H_2O is what we are,   } *twice*
H_2O clap hands, hurrah!
Water, water,
Water, water.   *(Clap or echo the word "water" after each word)*

Allocate parts to Molecules as appropriate: bullet points will indicate each new speaker.

- By the way, where are we?
- What do you mean?
- Well, are we in the sea, a river or what?
- Mmmmm . . . *tasting* . . . tastes salty.
- We must be in the sea today then.
- I see, the sea! Yippee!

Enter Seaside Children to sing the following song with actions suggested by the lyrics.

SONG TWO — A WAVE WENT UP MY NOSE

Verse 1:

Oh we do like to be swimming in the sea,
Splashing in the waves.
It's a wonderful feeling.
Bobbing up and down,
Wet from head to toes.
But if you hear me sneeze . . . ATCHOO!
A wave went up my nose.

Refrain:

Swim, swim, swim with me.
We like swimming in the deep blue sea.
When the sun's nice and hot,
We like swimming, a lot!

Verse 2:

Oh we do like to go paddling you know,
When we're by the sea.
It's a wonderful feeling.
Water all around,
Sand between your toes.
But if you hear me sneeze . . . ATCHOO!
A wave went up my nose.

Refrain:

Swim, swim, swim with me. . .

Repeat 1:

Oh we do like to be swimming in the sea,
Splashing in the waves.
It's a wonderful feeling.
Bobbing up and down,
Wet from head to toes.
But if you hear me sneeze . . . ATCHOO!
A wave went up my nose,
That's where it always goes.
Right, up, my, nose!
AAA . . A-TCHOO!

Exit Seaside Children.

- It's fun in the sea.
- I wonder where we'll go next?
- I don't know!
- It's getting very hot around here.

Enter Sun and Sunbeams.

7

Sunbeams: High in the sky the sun shines bright
                  Filling all the world with light.

Sun: Sunbeams dancing golden yellow
                  Warm the sparkling waves below.

SONG THREE   THE SUN HAS SAID GOODBYE TO MISTER MOON

Refrain: **The Sun has said goodbye to Mister Moon,
                  Night has gone away.
                  Goodbye Stars, it's time to go to bed,
                  It's a lovely day!
                  Hello Sunbeams, nice to see you now
                  You've come out to play.
                  Dance your sunny sunbeam dance because
                  It's a lovely day.**

Verse 1:   **Dance, dance, dance sunbeams,
                  Dance for the sun.
                  Dance, dance, dance sunbeams,
                  Dance for everyone.
                  Dance, dance, dance sunbeams,
                  Sparkling so bright.
                  Dance, dance, dance sunbeams,
                  In the morning light.**

Refrain: **The Sun has said goodbye to Mister Moon, . . .**

Verse 2:   **Oh please sun won't you
                  Shine every day?
                  Send your sunbeams to
                  Chase the clouds away.
                  When you're shining so
                  High in the sky.
                  We can sit and just
                  Let the world go by.**

Refrain: **The Sun has said goodbye to Mister Moon, . . .**

- Woh . . . . . ! We're going up.
- High as high!
- Up in the sky.
- Why?

Sunbeams: We're warming you up.
You're evaporating!
Turning you into clouds.

- Shout out loud,
  We're going to be a cloud!

- Here we go!
- Woh . . . . . !
- There are zillions and grillions of us left behind.
- Bye-bye sea.
- Bye-bye.

The Sunbeams exit after the Molecules, who pick up their cloud cardboard cut outs and re-enter the main acting area.

- Look, the earth is far away below us.
- I feel all misty.
- That's because we **are** all misty! We are clouds now.
- Water vapour.
- We've been water vapour before.
- Yes, once we were steam from a kettle.
- It must have been boiling!
- It was hot. Very, very hot!
- But we did make a nice cup of tea!

Enter Singing Groups to perform the next song.

SONG FOUR   **FIRE HEATS THE WATER**

Verse 1:   **Fire heats the water,**
                   Water gets so hot.
                   Turn the tap on, fill the kettle,
                   Got to boil it for the pot.
                   Tea, coffee, cocoa: now
                   What do you think?
                   If the water's cold,
                   Would they be so nice to drink?
                   No, no, no, no, I don't think so.
                   Oh no, no. I don't think so.

Verse 2:   **Fire heats the water,**
                   Water gets so hot.
                   Steam comes hissing from the kettle,
                   Pour the water in the pot.
                   Tea, coffee, cocoa: now
                   What do you think?
                   If the water's cold,
                   Would they be so nice to drink?
                   No, no, no, no, I don't think so.
                   Oh no, no. I don't think so.

Verse 3:   **Fire heats the water,**
                   Water gets so hot.
                   Add some sugar, cream or milk and
                   What a lovely drink you've got.
                   Tea, coffee, cocoa: now
                   What do you think?
                   If the water's cold,
                   Would they be so nice to drink?
                   No, no, no, no, I don't think so.
                   Oh no, no. I don't think so.

Exit Groups that have just sung.

(Cue 'wind' sound effect - refer to the CD. Fade out as required.)

- It's getting very windy up here.

Clouds start bumping into each other.

- Whoops!
- Sorry!
- Which way are we supposed to go?
- I don't know. The winds are arguing again. Listen to them.

Enter the Four Winds, vigorously arguing ("It's my turn!", "You've had your turn!" etc.)

East Wind: It's my turn to blow!

I'm the East Wind cruel and chill,
I'll freeze your skin and make you ill.
I'm the wind that whines and moans,
I'll bite your ears and freeze your bones.

North Wind: No! It's my turn. You blew all last week.

I'm the North Wind fierce and strong,
I blow hard and I blow long.
Blowing all the winter through
I bring frost and snow to you.

West Wind: Me, me me!

Hello, I don't think we've met,
I'm the West Wind, wild and wet.
I bring rain, and long ago
I blew ships 'round the world you know.

South Wind: Oh, I think you're much too rough,
Let me give a gentle puff!

I'm the South Wind, kind and warm,
I lightly blow and never storm.
And when the sun's too hot to bear,
I'll cool you with my gentle air.

All Winds: Me, me, me! My turn! My turn!
*Vigorously arguing
as before*

- Hey! Be careful!
- You'll blow us all to bits.

Enter TV Weather Presenter.

Presenter: Alright you lot,
Cut it out, all of you!
I'll tell you who blows next.

All Winds: You? That's a laugh.
You never get it right!

Presenter: Oh yes I do.

All Winds: Oh no you don't.

Presenter: Oh yes I do.
Turning to audience

Hopefully the audience responds in the time honoured way . . .

Presenter: I know exactly what you're going to do.
I've got satellites and all the latest technology.
So North Wind blow,
Away you go!

North Wind blows the other winds and the weather presenter off the stage, then turns his attention to the clouds and chases them around.

- Land ho!
- Look at those mountains.
- Over we go.
- Oh no, I'm starting to freeze.
- I'm turning to ice.
- I know, I know,
  We're going to snow!
- Oh great!
  We're going to precipitate!

Whispered softly • Down, down,
Drift to the ground.
Snowflakes fall
Without a sound.

The cloud cut outs are dispensed with and the North Wind exits.
Enter Snowflakes who dance and Winter Children who sing.

(The music is played three times on the CD. Allocate some part of the music to dance and some to singing as preferred.)

SONG FIVE	**SNOWFLAKES**

Verse 1:

Snowflakes, snowflakes,
Wonder how many
It takes to cover the ground.
See them turning,
Swirling, twirling
And whirling around and around.
Everyone waits for that beautiful sight,
When everything wears a carpet of white.
It's so enchanting, come on and let's go,
And play in the snow, snow, snow.

- Well, here we are. Now we're snow!
- We're something different wherever we go.
- Yes, but we're always water.
- And look who's coming.
- Well, isn't this nice?
  Here's old Jack Frost to turn us into ice.

Exit Snowflakes and enter Jack Frost and the Ice Fairies who sing the following song.

SONG SIX	**JACKY JACKY JACK FROST**

Verse 1:

Jacky Jacky Jack Frost bites my toes,
Jacky Jacky Jack Frost nips my nose.
Jacky Jacky Jack Frost thinks it's fun,
Freezing ev'rything and ev'ryone.

Verse 2:

Jacky Jacky Jack Frost waves his wand,
Freezes all the water in our pond.
Jacky Jacky Jack Frost thinks it's fun,
Freezing ev'rything and ev'ryone.

Verse 3:

He makes pretty patterns on the glass,
Fairy crystals where he passes.
It's such a really lovely sight,
Looking at the stars, on a cold and frosty chilly winter's night.

Verse 4: **Jacky Jacky Jack Frost thinks it's nice,**
Making ev'rything turn into ice.
Jacky Jacky Jack Frost thinks it's fun,
Freezing ev'rything and ev'ryone.

Sun and Sunbeams enter to instrumental reprise of Song Three.

- So now we're frozen solid,
  Hard as rock all round.

- We're pretty little snowflakes
  Frozen on the ground.

- Oooh! What was that I felt?
- Oh look. It's the sun.
- It's getting warmer, we're going to melt!
- Here come lots of clouds again.

An enormous clap of thunder heralds a thunder and lightning storm (refer to the CD). This acts as a cue for all characters to take a place on stage ready for the next song.

- Thunder and lightning!
- We're beginning to thaw!
- We're liquid again!
- The sun's to blame!
- Here we go, straight down the drain!
- Woh . . . . . . ! ! (*Enjoying the experience*)

SONG SEVEN   # THE HYDROLOGIC CYCLE RAG

Verse 1:

The rain, the rain goes down the drain,
Into the lakes and rivers again.
Sometimes it's a pain
To be soaked in rain,
But the rain fills up the sea.
And so there's plenty of H_2O,
That's our name for water, you know.
Plenty of H_2O for you and me.

Verse 2:

The hydrologic, hydrologic,
Hydrologic cycle my friend
Goes on for ever.
Now isn't that clever?
It's never ever going to end.
And so there's plenty of H_2O,
That's our name for water, you know.
Plenty of H_2O for you and me.

Verse 3:

First the sea evaporates,
Later on precipitates
Into hail, snow, sleet and rain,
Over and over and over and over and
Over and over and over again.

Repeat Verse 2:

The hydrologic, hydrologic,
Hydrologic cycle my friend
Goes on for ever.
Now isn't that clever?
It's never ever going to end.
And so there's plenty of H_2O,
That's our name for water, you know.
Plenty of H_2O for you and me.

Repeat Verse 1: **The rain, the rain goes down the drain,**
Into the lakes and rivers again.
Sometimes it's a pain
To be soaked in rain,
But the rain fills up the sea.
And so there's plenty of H_2O,
That's our name for water, you know.

Coda: **Plenty of H_2O for you and,**
Plenty of H_2O for you and,
Plenty of H_2O for you and me!

- Well now it's time to end our show.

- There's ever so much more to know,
  About this stuff called H_2O.

- There's water, water everywhere,
  In the ground and in the air.

- In the rivers, lakes and sea.
  There's even lots in you and me!

- Without it everything would die.
  All the oceans would run dry.

- So everyone before we go,
  Let's give a cheer for H_2O.

  Hip, hip, hooray!
  Hip, hip, hooray!
  Hip, hip, hooray!

ENCORE Repeat **THE HYDROLOGIC CYCLE RAG**
or any of the songs of your choice.

TEACHER'S NOTES

SONG ONE

H₂O

Atoms

Cue: . . . makes a water molecule!

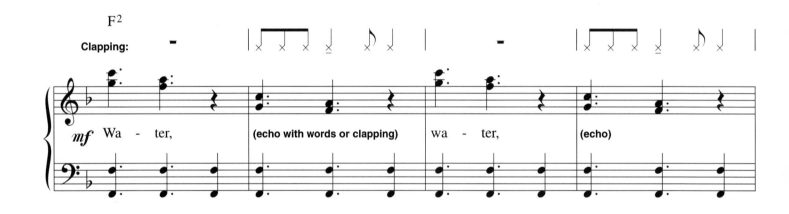

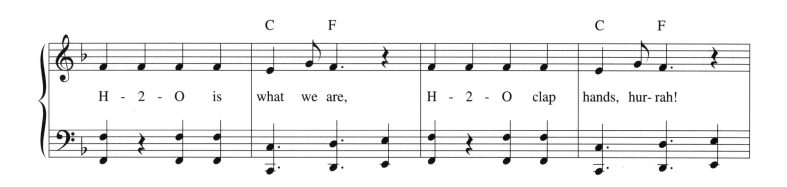

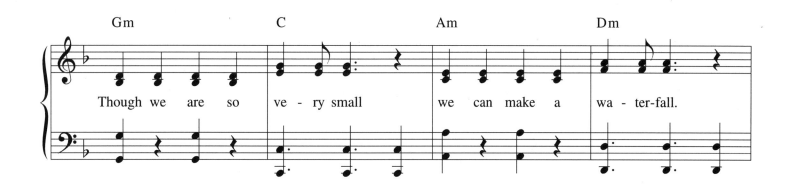

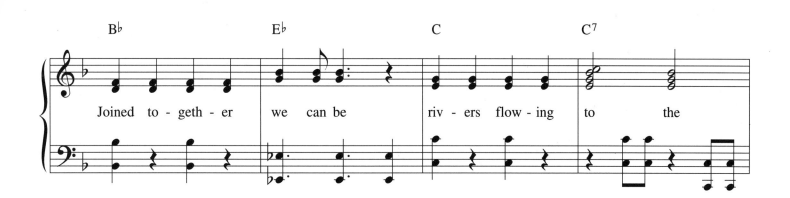

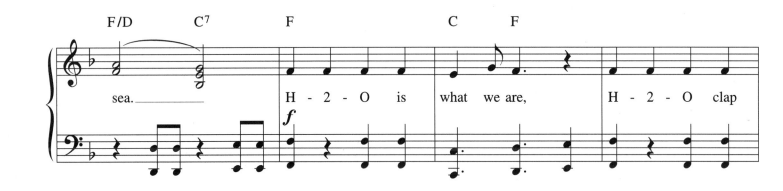

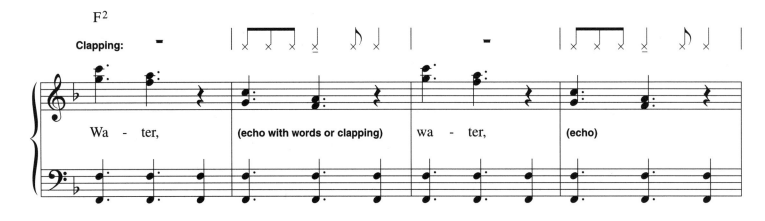

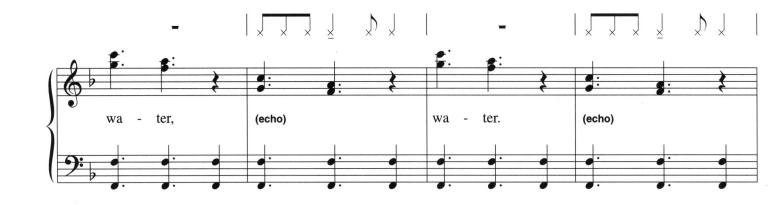

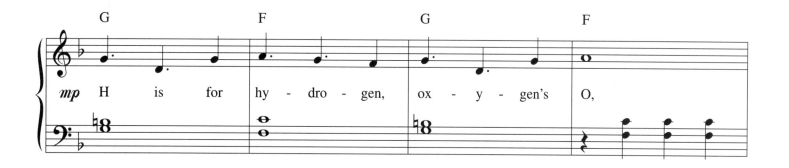

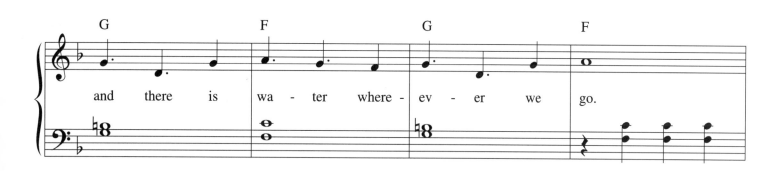

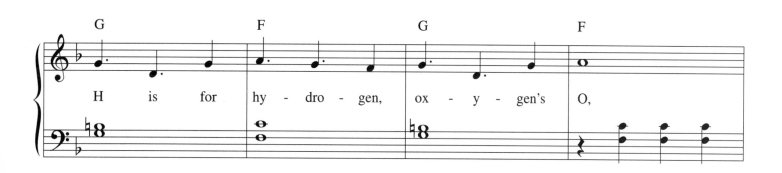

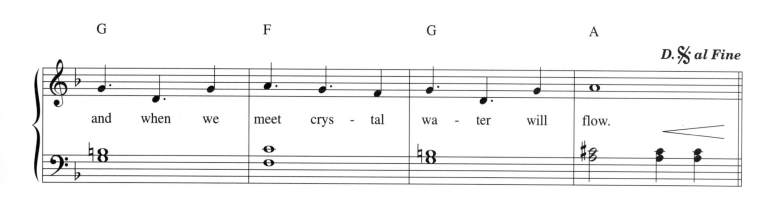

SONG TWO   # A WAVE WENT UP MY NOSE

Seaside Children

Cue: I see, the sea. Yippee!

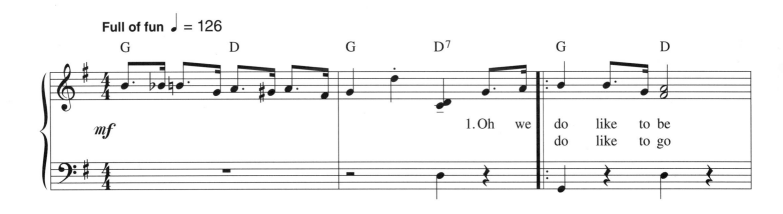

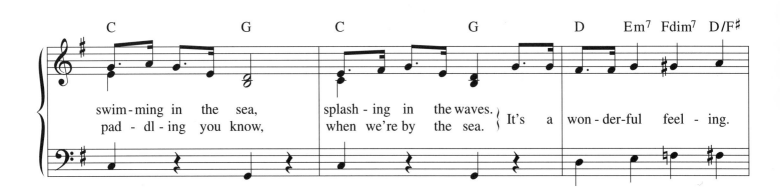

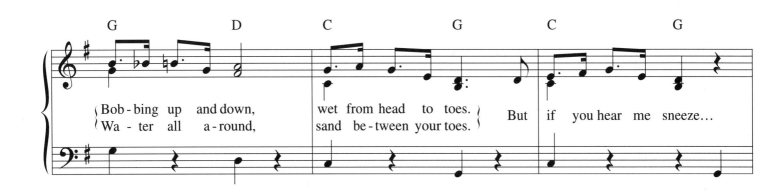

Refrain

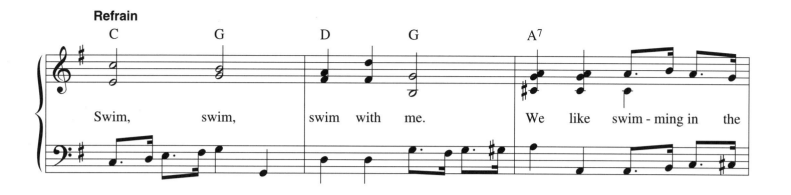

Swim, swim, swim with me. We like swim - ming in the

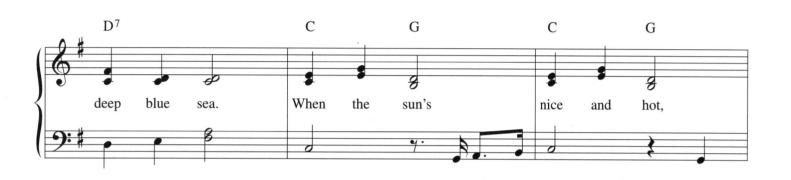

deep blue sea. When the sun's nice and hot,

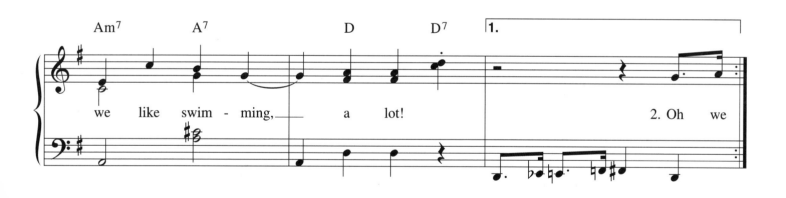

we like swim - ming, a lot!

2. Oh we

Repeat 1. Oh we do like to be swim - ming in the sea,

23

splash-ing in the waves. It's a won-der-ful feel-ing. Bob-bing up and down,

wet from head to toes. But if you hear me sneeze... A . . . .

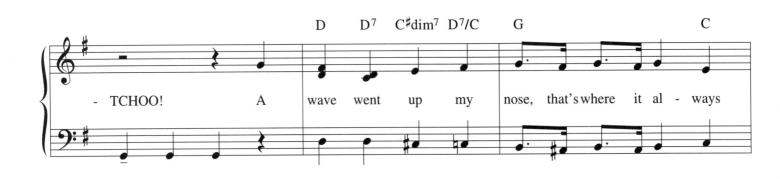

- TCHOO! A wave went up my nose, that's where it al - ways

goes. Right, up, my, nose! AAA . . . . A–TCHOO!

SONG THREE

THE SUN HAS SAID GOODBYE TO MISTER MOON

All

Cue: *Sunbeams dancing golden yellow*
Warm the sparkling waves below.

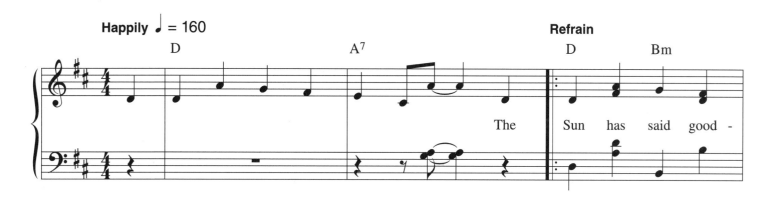

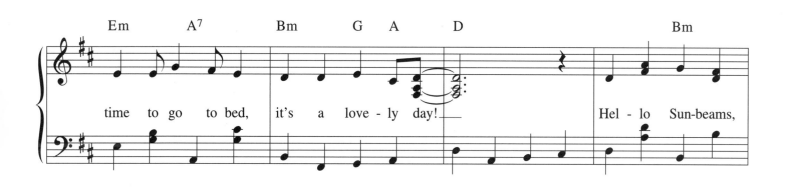

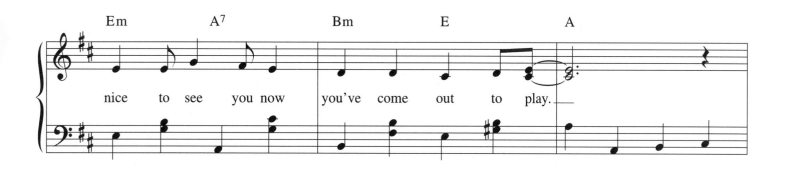

An instrumental version of this song is used later in the play for the re-entry of Sun and Sunbeams. This comes directly after Song Six JACKY JACKY JACK FROST.

SONG FOUR   FIRE HEATS WATER

Singing Groups

Cue: But we did make a nice cup of tea!

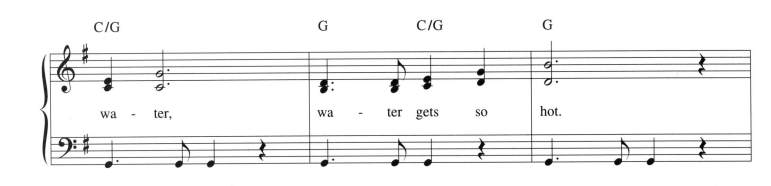

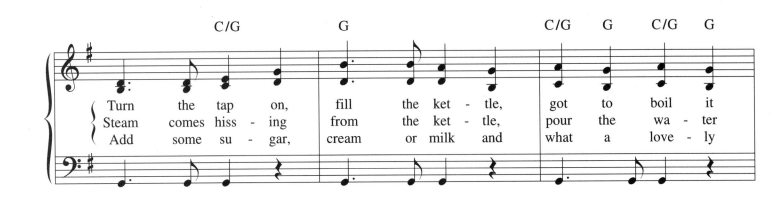

29

SONG FIVE

SNOWFLAKES

Winter Children

Cue: Snowflakes fall without a sound.

The music is played three times on the CD. Allocate some to dance and some to singing as preferred.
N.B. Voices sing an octave down from the notes given in the right hand piano music!

VOCAL LINE

SONG SIX   JACKY JACKY JACK FROST

Ice Fairies

Cue: Here's old Jack Frost to turn us into ice.

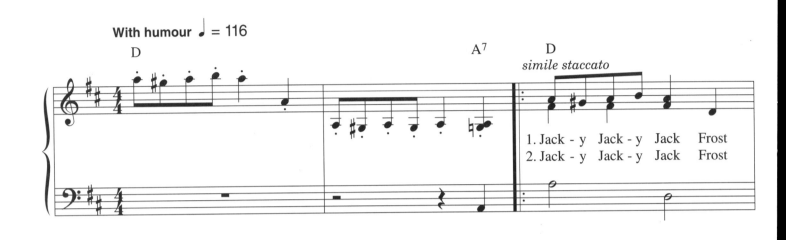

With humour ♩ = 116

1. Jack - y Jack - y Jack Frost
2. Jack - y Jack - y Jack Frost

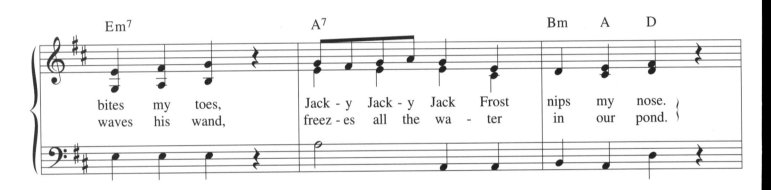

bites   my   toes,   Jack - y   Jack - y   Jack   Frost   nips   my   nose.
waves   his   wand,   freez - es   all   the   wa - ter   in   our   pond.

Jack - y Jack - y Jack Frost   thinks it's fun, freez - ing ev-'ry-thing and   ev - 'ry - one.

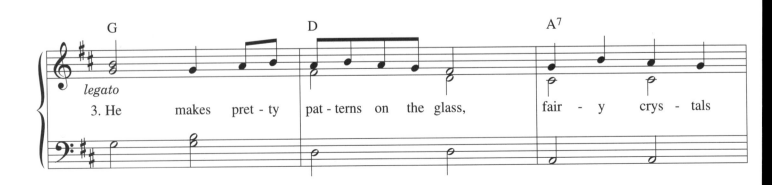

legato

3. He   makes   pret - ty   pat - terns   on   the   glass,   fair - y   crys - tals

An instrumental version of Song Three THE SUN HAS SAID GOODBYE TO MISTER MOON follows straight on from this song, for the re-entry of Sun and Sunbeams.

SONG SEVEN

THE HYDROLOGIC CYCLE RAG

All

Cue: Here we go, straight down the drain!
Woh . . . !!

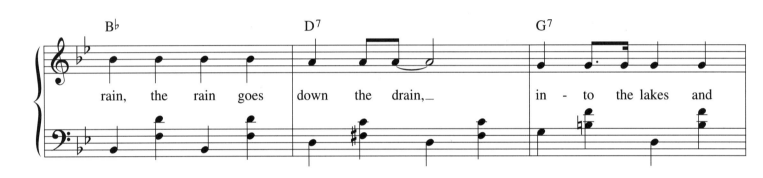

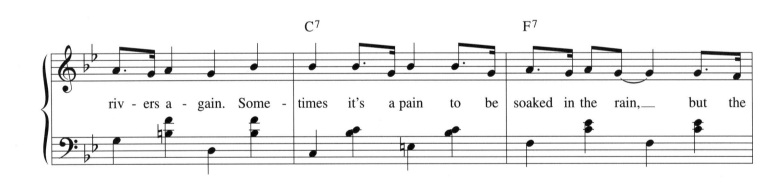

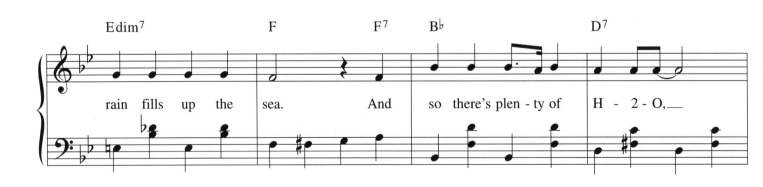

Lyrics from the score:

1. The rain, the rain goes down the drain,__ in - to the lakes and riv - ers a - gain. Some - times it's a pain to be soaked in the rain,__ but the rain fills up the sea. And so there's plen - ty of H - 2 - O,__

34

that's our name for wat - er, you know.__ Plen - ty of H - 2 -

- O for you and__ me._____ 2. The hy - dro - log - ic,

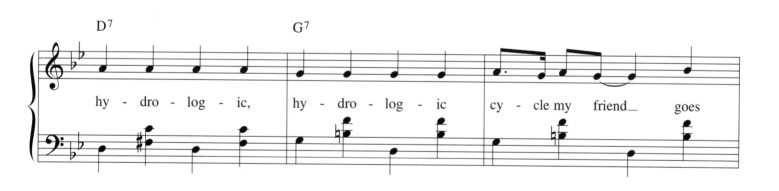

hy - dro - log - ic, hy - dro - log - ic cy - cle my friend__ goes

on for ev - er. Now is - n't that clev - er? It's nev - er ev - er go - ing to

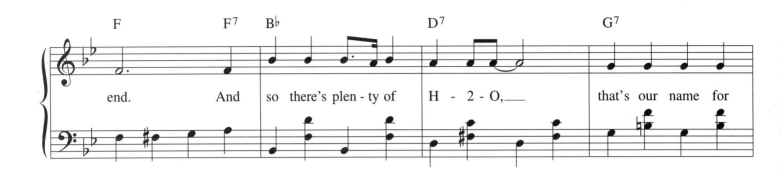

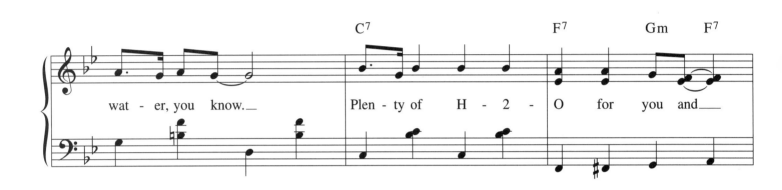

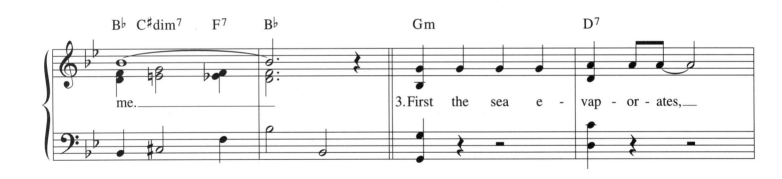

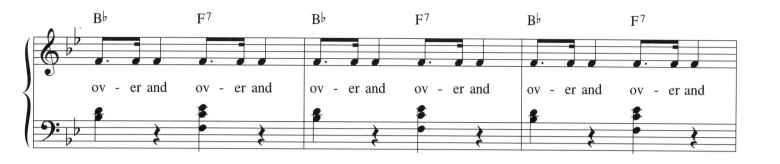

ov - er and ov - er and ov - er and ov - er and ov - er and ov - er and

ov - er a - gain.___ **Repeat** 2. The hy - dro - log - ic,

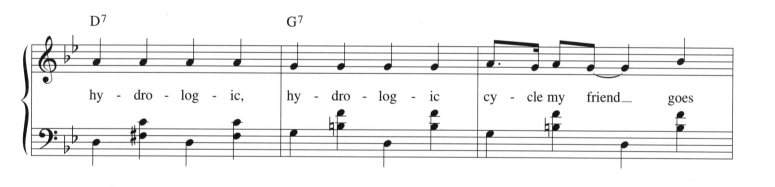

hy - dro - log - ic, hy - dro - log - ic cy - cle my friend___ goes

on for ev - er. Now is - n't that clev - er? It's nev - er ev - er go - ing to

37

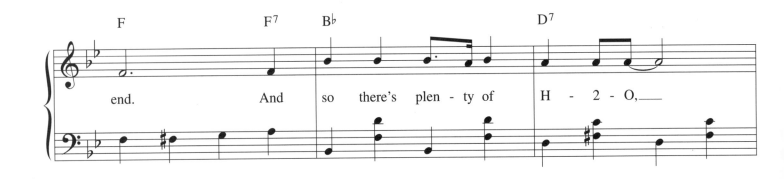

end. And so there's plen - ty of H - 2 - O,

that's our name for wat - er, you know. Plen - ty of H - 2 -

- O for you and me. **Repeat** 1. The rain, the rain goes

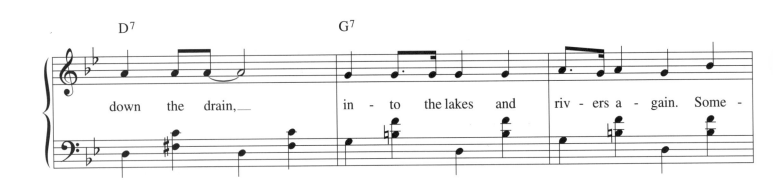

down the drain, in - to the lakes and riv - ers a - gain. Some -

CODA

Recent titles from Golden Apple!

Wormzzz! Takes the classroom down to a grass roots level, to look at nature from a more wriggly perspective! Containing seven brilliant new songs and dances by Douglas Wootton, this lively musical teaches children about the vital role worms play in nature.
Wormzzz! is ideal for topic work and can be used to support other areas of the curriculum. Comes with CD demonstration and backing tracks. Order No. GA11130

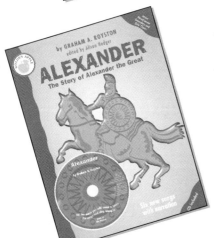

Alexander is a new musical by Graham A. Royston which includes six original songs describing the life and work of Alexander The Great. Aimed at Juniors, Mixed Lower Secondary and girls choirs. There is historical background information to go with each song and there are plenty of opportunities for class discussions on the subject. This book includes a map of Alexander's Route. Perfect for complementing history class. Comes with CD demonstration and backing tracks.
Alexander- Pupil's Book: - Order No. GA11286
Alexander- Teacher's Book: - Order No. GA11275

Happy Hat Land is a place where EVERYONE wears a hat! The Happy Hat folk are always happy, until one day a Hat Seller visits them bringing with him the most beautiful, stunning silver hat they have ever seen! Of course, everyone wants the silver hat and they argue for a whole week, trying to decide who gets it. The Hat Seller returns to teach them a game that shows them how to share, so everyone gets a turn at wearing the silver hat and the people of Happy Hat Land are happy once more! This musical carries a strong moral message about sharing, and how it can be fun! Aimed at Pre-school, KS1 and special needs children. Comes with CD demonstration and backing tracks. Written by Niki Davies.
Order No. GA11297

Scarecrow's Christmas by Alison Hedger is all about putting the needs of others before yourself. Scarecrow doesn't have many clothes and as a result is very cold in winter. Many different animals try and give him their coats- Polar Bears, Ducklings and even Silver Fish, but Scarecrow always gives them away to those in greater need than himself.
Aimed at children ages 4 and 8.
Comes with CD with demonstration and backing tracks plus wintry sound effect.
Order No. GA11363